AMERICAN ★★★ ICONS

Uncle Sam

Helen Lepp Friesen

LET'S READ

AV²

BY WEIGL™

ADDED VALUE • AUDIO VISUAL

Go to **www.av2books.com**, and enter this book's unique code.

BOOK CODE

U378551

AV² by Weigl brings you media enhanced books that support active learning.

AV² provides enriched content that supplements and complements this book. Weigl's AV² books strive to create inspired learning and engage young minds in a total learning experience.

Your AV² Media Enhanced books come alive with...

Audio
Listen to sections of the book read aloud.

Video
Watch informative video clips.

Embedded Weblinks
Gain additional information for research.

Try This!
Complete activities and hands-on experiments.

Key Words
Study vocabulary, and complete a matching word activity.

Quizzes
Test your knowledge.

Slide Show
View images and captions, and prepare a presentation.

... and much, much more!

Published by AV² by Weigl
350 5th Avenue, 59th Floor New York, NY 10118
Website: www.av2books.com   www.weigl.com

Library of Congress Control Number: 2012940130

ISBN 978-1-61913-081-4 (hard cover)
ISBN 978-1-61913-304-4 (soft cover)

Printed in the United States of America in North Mankato, Minnesota
2 3 4 5 6 7 8 9 0 16 15 14 13 12

112012
WEP281112

Editor: Aaron Carr   Design: Mandy Christiansen

Photo Credits
Every reasonable effort has been made to trace ownership and to obtain permission to reprint copyright material. The publishers would be pleased to have any errors or omissions brought to their attention so that they may be corrected in subsequent printings.

Weigl acknowledges Getty Images as the primary image supplier for this title. Page 14 photo by Matt H. Wade.

CONTENTS

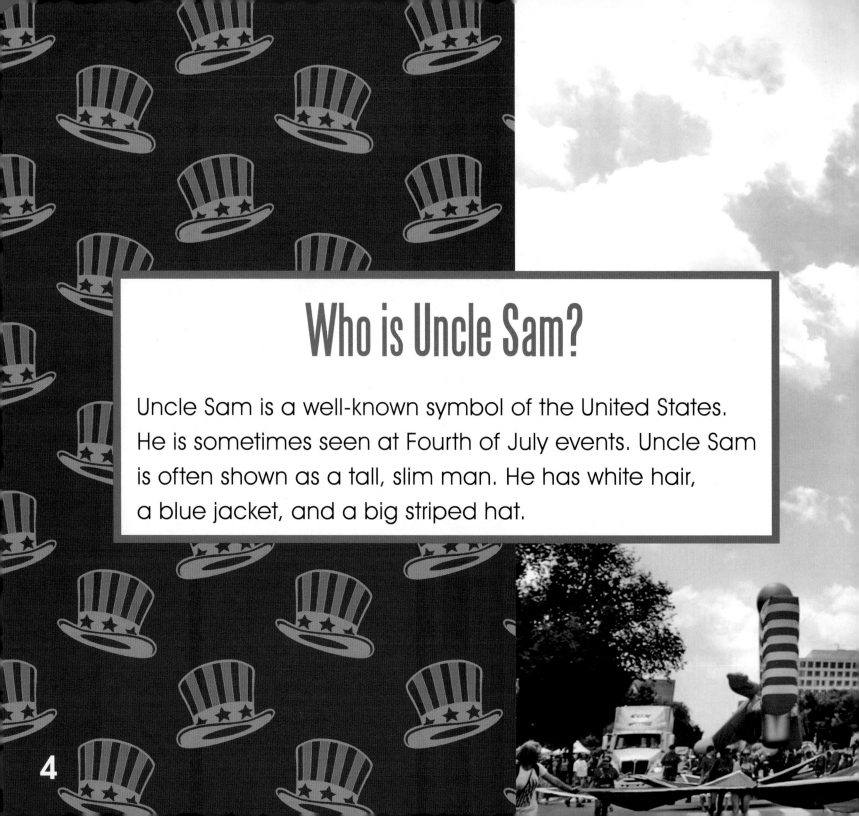

Who is Uncle Sam?

Uncle Sam is a well-known symbol of the United States. He is sometimes seen at Fourth of July events. Uncle Sam is often shown as a tall, slim man. He has white hair, a blue jacket, and a big striped hat.

A National Symbol

Uncle Sam's clothes are red, white, and blue. These are the colors of the American flag. Uncle Sam often stands for the United States and its people.

The Real Uncle Sam

The symbol of Uncle Sam came from a real man. His name was Samuel Wilson.

SAMUEL ★ WILSON

1766 - 1854

Who was Samuel Wilson?

Samuel Wilson sent meat from his shop to soldiers during the War of 1812. The meat was packed in barrels marked "U.S." This stood for United States.

Becoming an Icon

Soldiers started to say that "U.S." stood for Uncle Sam. They said the meat came from Uncle Sam. A newspaper wrote a story about Uncle Sam. Uncle Sam soon became a nickname for the United States.

14

Home of Uncle Sam

Samuel Wilson's meat company was in Troy, New York. Today, Troy is known as the home of Uncle Sam.

Uncle Sam in Art

Many artists made pictures of Uncle Sam. The first pictures of Uncle Sam looked like Samuel Wilson.

17

Uncle Sam Posters

James Montgomery Flagg drew the most famous poster of Uncle Sam. The poster was made to get more people to join the army. In the picture, Uncle Sam points his finger. He says, "I want you for U.S. Army."

Uncle Sam Today

Today, Uncle Sam can be seen in newspaper cartoons, on posters, and in parades. Uncle Sam is an official symbol of the United States.

21

UNCLE SAM FACTS

These pages provide detailed information that expands on the interesting facts found in the book. These pages are intended to be used by adults as a learning support to help young readers round out their knowledge of each national symbol featured in the *American Icons* series.

Pages 4–5

Who is Uncle Sam? Uncle Sam is a symbol of the United States. A symbol is an image or picture that stands for something else. Uncle Sam is often used to represent the United States government. Cartoons and posters usually show Uncle Sam as a tall, slim, elderly man with stern eyes and white hair.

Pages 6–7

A National Symbol Uncle Sam wears clothes that represent the American flag. Most commonly, he wears a red and white striped top hat with white stars on blue trim. His goatee beard is pointy and white. He wears a white shirt with a red bow tie under a blue coat. Red and white striped pants finish the outfit.

Pages 8–9

The Real Uncle Sam The real Uncle Sam was a man named Samuel Wilson. He worked as a meat packer. During the War of 1812, Samuel Wilson was eager to help his country. He contributed to the war by providing beef for the soldiers to eat.

Pages 10–11

Who was Samuel Wilson? Samuel Wilson and his brother Ebenezer opened a company called E. & S. Wilson. Their company earned a contract to provide meat to the U.S. Army. They packed the meat in barrels and marked each with the letters "U.S." This showed that the barrels were for the United States government.

Becoming an Icon People in Samuel Wilson's hometown sometimes called him Uncle Sam When soldiers saw "U.S." marked on the barrels, they said the meat shipments came from Uncle Sam. A local newspaper ran a story about this. Soon, Uncle Sam became a nickname for the United States government.

Home of Uncle Sam By 1813, Uncle Sam had become known across the country. On May 12, 1830, the New York *Gazette* printed a story connecting Samuel Wilson to the Uncle Sam character. Samuel Wilson's hometown of Troy, New York, is still known as the home Uncle Sam. Samuel Wilson is buried in the Oakwood Cemetery in Troy.

Uncle Sam in Art Many artists drew pictures of Uncle Sam. Some people thought the original cartoon of Uncle Sam looked like Samuel Wilson. In the 1860s, a political cartoonist named Thomas Nast popularized the image of Uncle Sam with a white beard. Later, cartoons did not resemble Samuel Wilson anymore.

Uncle Sam Posters In 1916, James Montgomery Flagg drew the best-known poster of Uncle Sam. In the poster, Uncle Sam points his finger and says, "I want you for U.S. Army." During World War I, more than four million posters were printed. They were used to recruit soldiers for the army. Flagg used his own face as the basis for his drawing of Uncle Sam.

Uncle Sam Today In 1961, the United States Congress officially recognized Samuel Wilson as the man behind the American icon, Uncle Sam. The image of Uncle Sam has remained mostly unchanged since the 1960s.

KEY WORDS

Research has shown that as much as 65 percent of all written material published in English is made up of 300 words. These 300 words cannot be taught using pictures or learned by sounding them out. They must be recognized by sight. This book contains 54 common sight words to help young readers improve their reading fluency and comprehension. This book also teaches young readers several important content words, such as nouns. These words are paired with pictures to aid in learning and improve understanding.

Page	Sight Words First Appearance
4	a, and, as, at, big, has, he, is, man, of, often, sometimes, the, well, white, who
7	American, are, for, its, people, these
8	came, from, his, name, was
11	in, this, to
12	about, an, said, say, soon, started, story, that
15	home
16	first, like, made, many, pictures
19	get, I, more, most, points, want, you
20	be, can, on

Page	Content Words First Appearance
4	events, hair, hat, jacket, Uncle Sam, United States
7	clothes, colors, flag
8	Samuel Wilson
11	barrels, meat, shop, soldiers, War of 1812
12	icon, newspaper, nickname
15	company, New York, Troy
16	art, artists
19	army, finger, James Montgomery Flagg, posters
20	cartoons, parades

Check out www.av2books.com for activities, videos, audio clips, and more!

1 Go to www.av2books.com.

2 Enter book code. | U 3 7 8 5 5 1 |

3 Fuel your imagination online!

www.av2books.com